Kids' Guide

Local Government

Ernestine Giesecke

Heinemann Library
Chicago, Illinois

Customer Service 888-454-2279
www.heinemannlibrary.com

Designed by Jennifer Carney
Printed in Hong Kong

04 03 02 01
10 9 8 7 6 5 4 3 2

Library of Congress Cataloging-In-Publication Data
Giesecke, Ernestine, 1945-
    Local government / Ernestine Giesecke.
        p. cm. – (Kids' guide)
    Includes bibliographical references and index.
    Summary: Introduces the purpose and function of local governments, explores the three
    branches of government at the city and county level, and presents the relationships
    between city and suburban governments and between various governments and schools.
    ISBN 1-57572-512-6 (library binding)
    1. Local government--United States—Juvenile literature. [1. Local government. 2.
    United States—Politics and government.] I. Title. II. Series.
    JS331.G54 2000
    320.473—dc21   99-057612

Acknowledgments
The publishers would like to thank the following for permission to reproduce photographs:
The Granger Collection, p. 5; Paul Conklin/Monkmeyer Press, p. 7; Bob Daemmrich pp., 8, 9;
Michael Brosilow for Heinemann Library, pp. 10, 21; T. Savina/Gamma-Liaison, p. 12; Los
Angeles County Sheriffs Department, p. 13; Sidney/Monkmeyer Press, p. 18; Bob
Daemmrich/Uniphoto, p. 19; Spencer Grant/Photo Edit, p. 20; David Young-Wolff/Photo Edit,
p. 22; Shackman/Monkmeyer Press, p.23; Ed Kashi, p. 24; C.J. Allen/Stock Boston, p. 25;
Grantpix/Monkmeyer Press, p. 26; Bob Daemmrich/Stock Boston.

Cover: Spencer Grant/Photo Edit

The publisher would like to thank Susan Temple, of the North Carolina Department of Public
Instruction, and Jay Adler for their comments in the preparation of this book.

Note to the reader: Some words are shown in bold, **like this.**
You can find out what they mean by looking in the glossary.

Contents

What Is Government?

A government is the organization of people that directs the actions of a nation, state, or community. A government has the **authority** and power to make, carry out, and **enforce** laws. It can also settle disagreements about those laws.

In the United States, the government's power comes from the U.S. Constitution. The Constitution is a **document** that describes, or identifies, the powers of the government. It also places limits on those powers.

National Powers	State Powers	Local Powers
Make agreements with other nations	Vote on constitutional amendments	Make agreements with state and other local governments
Provide for national defense	Make agreements with other states and the national and local governments	Preserve law and order
Collect **taxes** on goods from other countries	Hold **elections,** decide voting requirements	Keep legal records
Print **currency, mint** coins	Keep powers not given to the national government	Keep powers not assigned to state or national government

*Since colonial times, voters have attended town meetings. At these meetings, people of the town meet with **officials** to discuss the responsibilities of the town toward its citizens.*

Governments, including the government of the United States of America, have many purposes. The most important purpose is to make the laws under which the people live. People need to know what is expected of them and what they should expect of their government.

One thing that people should expect is that their government will protect them. In a community, the government organizes the police and fire departments. In a nation, the government organizes the military, such as an army, navy, or air force, to protect them from other nations.

Many nations regard protecting the rights of an individual as an important purpose of government. In the United States, the Constitution lets each person believe what he or she wishes. It gives people the right to hold meetings and express opinions—even if these opinions disagree with actions of the government.

Local Government

In the United States, each state has a written constitution that describes both the powers of the state's government and how its powers should be **enforced.** State constitutions are much more detailed than the U.S. Constitution. They contain exact descriptions of what state **officials** may do—and how they should do it. State constitutions even describe how the local governments should be set up.

Nearly all the states in the United States are divided into counties to simplify governing millions of people. There are more than 3,000 counties in the United States. Rhode Island has only 5 counties, but Iowa has more than 90.

The state of Louisiana calls its counties parishes. Alaska calls its counties boroughs.

0	24 miles
0	40 km

Rhode Island

Some states have many counties, while others have just a few.

0	75 miles
0	125 km

Iowa

These members of a Navajo tribe meet to set up rules and laws that will affect those living on tribal lands.

People living in **rural** areas, outside of cities and on farms, usually depend on county governments for protection, roads, and other **benefits.** Many rural areas are divided into townships. Decisions affecting areas smaller than counties may be made by township governments.

From the east coast west to Nebraska, Kansas, and the Dakotas, the jobs of rural local government are shared by counties and townships. Counties are the major units of government in rural areas in much of the South and West.

Native Americans, living on lands set aside for their use, often depend on a local tribal government. The tribal government has the **authority** and power to make and **enforce** laws for the members of the tribe living on tribal lands. The tribal government also has the authority to make agreements with the **federal** government.

County Responsibilities

County governments do many jobs for the people living in the county by representing the state. Counties help protect an individual's rights by **enforcing** state and **federal** laws, keeping the peace, and maintaining jails. Counties have courts, so that disagreements about the law can be worked out and people who may have done something against the law can be **tried.**

This county health department worker checks food to make sure that it is not contaminated.

County agricultural agents work with farmers to develop the best ways to farm based on weather and soil conditions in the county.

Much of what a county does is for the common good—for all the people living in the county. County health departments require **vaccinations** for school children. They may even require vaccinations for dogs and cats so that people can be protected from certain diseases. Some counties provide water, **sewer,** or electrical service. A county may provide police or fire protection.

Other people working for the county decide which roads need repairs and what the speed limit will be on streets and roads in the county. Some counties test automobile engines to be sure they are not adding to air pollution. County governments also may build bridges, storm drains, airports, parks, libraries, and schools.

Counties can be very different in **population.** Loving County, Texas, has 140 **residents**. Los Angeles County, California, is home to 9.1 million people.

Counties also keep official records. These include **deeds** to property, birth certificates, and marriage licenses.

9

County Government

Most counties are run by a group of people called the county board. The members of the board, often known as commissioners, are elected by the people living in the county. The board may have three or five members, who are usually elected to serve a **term** of four years.

You can get a copy of your birth certificate from the county clerk in the county in which you were born.

The *sheriff* is another county official who may be elected. He or she is in charge of the county jail and provides police protection for **rural** areas that are not covered by city or town police. Part of the sheriff's job is to carry out orders from the local court, such as removing people from a house when they have not been paying their rent.

The *county clerk* registers and records each change of land ownership in the county. The clerk also keeps a record of the births, deaths, marriages, and divorces in the county.

The *county assessor* sets the value of plots of land in the county. This value is used to tell property owners how much property **tax** they have to pay to keep the county and its schools and libraries functioning.

The *county auditor* keeps track of all the money the county takes in and pays the county's bills.

The *district attorney* is the county's lawyer. He or she investigates crimes and decides when individuals should be charged. The district attorney also **prosecutes** the cases in court.

The *county coroner* investigates some deaths, especially those that occur as a result of accident or violence. If a person dies without being under a doctor's care, the county coroner tries to find out the cause of the death.

The *county surveyor* **surveys** land and sets boundary lines. This job is important when new roads are being built, or in places where the land changes because of earthquakes, landslides, or flooding. The surveyor records how any boundary lines may have moved.

Local Government in Action

Many of the jobs county governments do are the same no matter where the county is located. Some counties, however, have taken on special jobs related to the needs of the county **residents.**

Counties may work on special local problems caused by weather, the conditions of the land, or the needs of their residents.

People in Florida, for example, often face hurricanes and tropical storms. Pinellas County, Florida, put together a book about hurricanes. It tells residents about the danger of the storms, what to do if they have to leave their homes, and ways they can make sure their pets are safe during a storm.

One of the jobs of local government is to help residents who have been affected by natural disasters.

The bicycle this teen is repairing will soon provide transportation for a child.

The Los Angeles, California, Sheriff's Department has begun a bicycle program. Volunteers teach young people how to repair bikes that have been lost or stolen and never reclaimed. When the bikes are repaired, they are given to needy children in the county.

Many homes in McHenry County, Illinois, get their drinking water from wells. If the ground over a well is flooded, the water may not be safe to drink. McHenry County will test water from flooded wells at no charge.

Each year, the Traffic Commission in York County, Virginia, makes up a map showing where the most traffic accidents occurred during the past year. The map is mailed to every home in the county. Drivers learn where they need to drive with extra care.

City Governments

Most of the people in the United States live in cities. Each city has a form of government that protects and serves the people living in the city. City governments are one kind of **municipal** government. Some states have slightly different governments for areas called villages or towns. This map shows the U.S. cities with the largest **populations.**

Each city's existence has been approved by its state. Each city has a **charter**—an agreement giving the people in the city the power to govern themselves. The kinds of control that states may have over the cities within their boundaries are different for each state.

Cities are the population centers of the state. In Illinois, for example, nearly one-fourth of the people live in the city of Chicago.

CANADA

ME

VT

NH

NY

MA • Boston

CT RI

WI

MI

Milwaukee•

Detroit•

• New York City

Chicago•

PA

Philadelphia•

NJ

• Pittsburgh

IL

Indianapolis•

Columbus•

MD

DE

O

Washington, DC ✪

Atlantic Ocean

as City

IN

WV

St. Louis•

VA

MO

KY

NC

TN

Charlotte•

AR

• Memphis

SC

• Atlanta

MS

AL

GA

LA

Jacksonville•

New Orleans•

FL

Miami•

United States

✪	National Capital
Seattle•	City
——	International Boundary
——	State Boundary
TX	State Name

0   400 kilometers

0   400 Miles

Gulf of Mexico

City Responsibilities

Cities have many of the same responsibilities as counties and states. City governments must make sure that **residents** are safe and protected from crime and disease. Residents also must have good housing, education, and transportation. Cities often help businesses get started. Finally, city government must keep records.

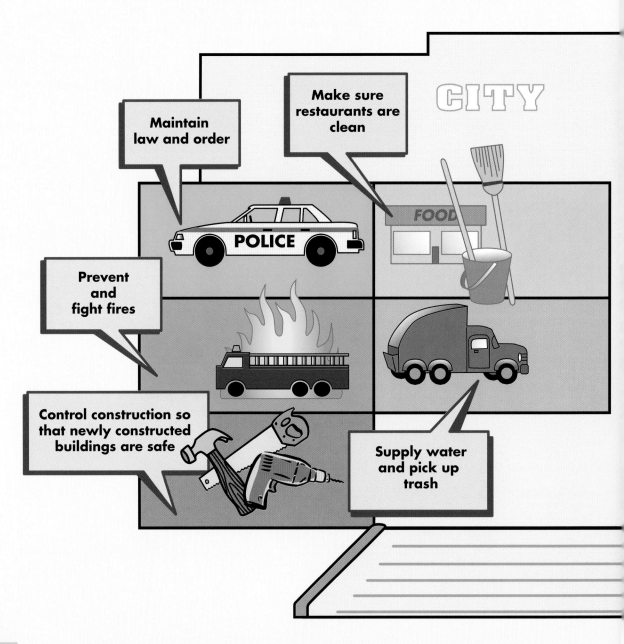

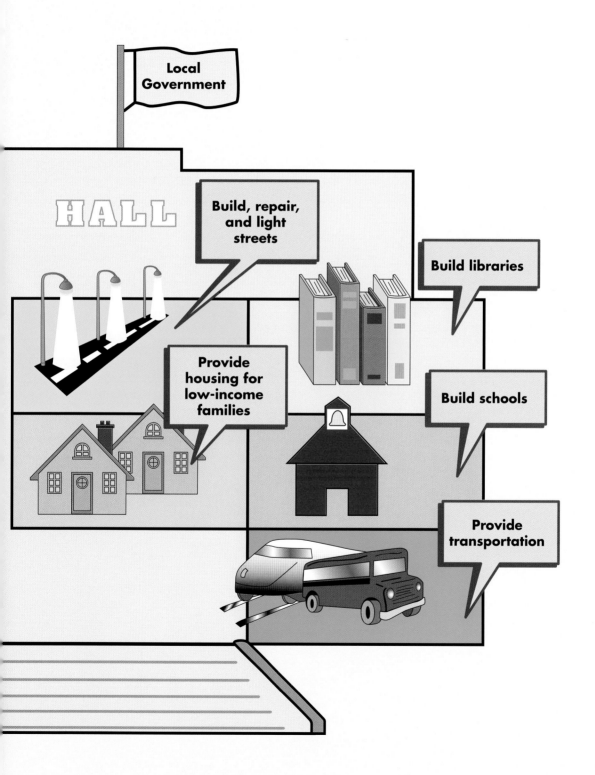

More City Jobs

Today's city governments spend much of their time and money on health and education. They provide clinics and hospitals for people who may not be able to afford doctors or medicine. They offer special health care for older people. Cities often have programs that help both children and adults who have physical or mental disabilities.

Caring for children is a task for both city and county governments. Many cities have agencies that work to find caring homes for children whose parents have died or who have **neglected** them.

City governments provide garbage removal as part of their efforts to protect the health of the **residents.**

As part of the common good, cities often offer recreational and educational facilities such as museums or music festivals.

If a city is large enough, it may provide transportation services. Usually taxicabs require **licenses** issued by the city. Cities often have buses and trains that bring people to and from work or shopping each day. Larger cities may even build and take care of airports.

Cities provide water to homes and businesses. Other **utilities,** such as gas for heating and cooking and electricity for light, are generally provided by privately owned companies, but the cities keep a close watch on the companies. Cities, as well as states, make sure that the utility companies provide reliable service at a fair price.

City governments want to make their cities attractive places to live. They may provide public parks and playgrounds, golf courses, and even zoos. Big cities may have museums, planetariums, aquariums, and art galleries.

City Mayors and Councils

Most cities in the United States have a government that is headed by a mayor and a city council. Both the mayor and the council members are elected to office.

The mayor is the head of the city government. It is his or her job to make sure that ideas and laws that make the city a good place to live, work, and play are carried out.

A mayor reports to the city council on how well the city is doing its job and what improvements the city government needs to make.

The city council is a group of people who work with the mayor to govern the city. The number of people on a city council can vary greatly. In some cities, the city council passes city **ordinances.** For example, a city council might pass an ordinance that forbids skateboarding on the city's main streets.

In some cities, the mayor has great **authority.** He or she can veto, or stop, an ordinance passed by the city council. This is true in cities such as Boston, New York City, Chicago, and Philadelphia.

In such cities, the mayor usually prepares the budget, or spending plan, for the city. The city council reviews the mayor's plan for spending the city's money and votes on whether to accept it.

A strong mayor can also appoint people to be the police or fire chief. He or she may name people to lead other city agencies, such as the health department or streets and roads. A strong mayor can also dismiss these people.

In other cities, the city council is more powerful than the mayor. In this case, the mayor acts as the chairperson of the council. He or she also represents the city at public events, such as parades.

In some cities, city council members are known as aldermen.

City Managers

S ome city governments are organized like large companies. These cities are run by a businessperson called a city manager.

These cities usually have a small elected city council and may also have a mayor, but most of the work of running the city is done by the city manager. The city council **hires** the city manager.

The city manager's job is described in the city's **charter.** He or she prepares the budget, appoints people to important jobs in the city, and oversees the work of city departments. The city manager also attends and takes part in city council meetings and may even propose subjects to discuss. In a manager-council city government, the council is not allowed to interfere with the job of the city manager.

A person living in a city might be governed by several different governments—the city government for parking, water, and police; the county government for schools, parks, and public transportation; and the state government for fishing in state forest preserves and driving regulations.

This is the city council for Los Angeles, California.

City council meetings are usually open to the public, so that residents can participate in their local government.

When a city with a city manager also has a mayor, the mayor is usually **elected** by the city council. He or she leads the council meetings and represents the city at important events. Cities with a city manager-council government include Des Moines, Iowa, and Cincinnati, Ohio.

Suburbs and Towns

A suburb is a community outside—but close to—a city. Just as with city government, a suburb's existence is approved by the state. Suburbs follow the same state rules and regulations that major cities follow. Suburbs can have the same kinds of governments that cities have.

Usually, suburban and city governments work together. They try to provide public transportation between the suburbs and the city. They may share the responsibility for some roads and highways.

In the suburbs, people often commute several miles from their homes to their jobs.

Businesses in many cities depend on suburbanites who come into the city each day to work.

Suburbs and the cities they surround depend on one another. The city depends on people from the suburbs to fill many of the jobs located in the city. People in the suburbs often depend on the city for recreation, medical help, and advanced education.

Beyond the suburbs are towns and villages. They are generally smaller than cities. They, too, are subject to the state's rules. Towns are often governed by a mayor and a town council.

In New England, many towns have a form of government called the town meeting. Voters get together at least once a year and make important decisions that affect everyone in the town, such as setting **taxes** and passing **ordinances.**

Electing City Government

In cities, as in most states, there are two major **political parties.** A political party is a group of people who have similar views about government. Most of the people who run, or try to win **election,** for state office belong to either of the two major political parties—Democratic or Republican. There are also many smaller parties.

In many cities, the basic unit of government is the **precinct.** Several precincts make up a region called a ward. The people in each ward usually elect a person to be on the city council. In some cities, these **officials** are called aldermen. City **residents** often ask their ward leaders directly for things they need, such as better garbage pickup or more police protection. Or they may ask that a section of street or alley be repaired.

*While **campaigning** for city office, candidates work hard to meet people and find out what they expect from city government.*

Many people work on a campaign to make sure that the voters know who the candidate is and what he or she will do if elected.

Ward leaders and other people interested in being a part of city government must campaign for the job. A good candidate listens to what the voters living in the city have to say about things that should be changed. Candidates promise that if they are elected they will try to make the changes that the voters want.

Paying for Local Government

City and county services cost money. Street cleaners and mayors each need to be paid for their work. City buses and trains need to be purchased, maintained, and repaired. These things are paid for from money collected as **taxes.**

Different cities and counties use different ways of raising money. A county board can collect taxes and borrow money for the county. Most of the money to run county government comes from taxes on property that people own. Some cities and counties also have a sales tax, which is collected on some purchases.

Cities and counties also have other sources of money. For example, most cities require a person planning to build within the city to get a building **permit.** The fees paid for this permit help the city keep track of construction to be sure that it is done properly and that the buildings are safe.

Some cities place a tax on the cost of a hotel room. This helps the city provide services for people who stay only a few days in the city.

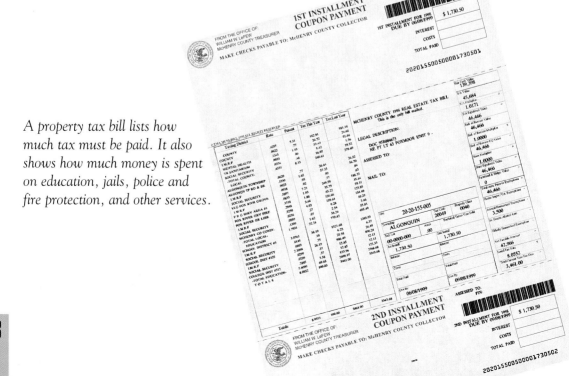

A property tax bill lists how much tax must be paid. It also shows how much money is spent on education, jails, police and fire protection, and other services.

28

Schools: A Special Case

There are more than 15,000 public school districts in the United States. School districts may include one or many schools. They are set up by state governments, but local governments oversee their day-to-day operation.

In many school districts, a board of education decides what the students will study, who will teach in the schools, and how the school buildings will be maintained. Members of the board of education are sometimes elected by the people. The members of the board choose a superintendent to be in charge of the schools in the district. In some places, both the school board and the superintendent are appointed, or chosen, by a mayor.

Federal, state, and local governments work together to provide free public education. In many places, most money to pay for schools comes from property **tax.** Many people feel that method is unfair because areas with higher property values receive more money for schools than do areas with lower property values. Local and state governments are looking for other ways to pay for public schools.

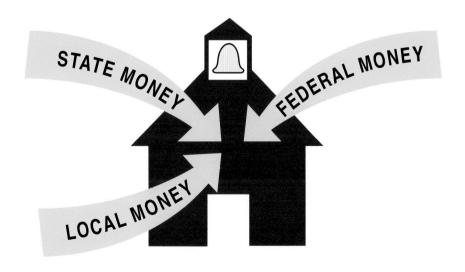

Finding Local Government

You can use the library and newspapers to find out about the local government where you live. The telephone book lists city departments and their telephone numbers. This may be in a special section at the front or in the middle of the book. You can also ask your librarian for help in finding out if your city, town, or county has a website on the Internet.

Glossary

authority power to enforce laws, command obedience, or judge

benefit something provided by a government to its citizens, such as health care, education, housing, or retirement income

campaign organized effort to win election to public office

candidate person who wants to be elected to a political office

charter paper granting cities the right to self-government

currency paper money or coins that are used in a country

deed paper that proves ownership of property

document written or printed paper

election process of making a choice by voting

enforce to make people obey

federal referring to a group of states that give up some power to a central government, also referring to the central government of the United States

hire to select someone to do a job for pay instead of holding an election

license legal permission to do something such as drive a car or get married

mint to manufacture coins

municipal relating to a place, usually fairly small, with self government

neglected not taken care of properly

official elected or appointed person in a position of power

ordinance city rule or law

permit paper or card that shows permission to do something

political party group of people who have similar views about government

population total number of people who live in a certain area

precinct smallest political division, where voting takes place

prosecute to attempt to prove a person guilty of a crime

resident person who lives in a community

rural located away from a city, in the country

sewer underground pipe to carry away waste

survey to measure the area or boundary of a piece of land

tax fee paid to a government, based on property value, earnings, or purchases

term length of time, set by law, that is served by an elected person

try to establish guilt or innocence in a court of law

utility public service such as water, gas, or electricity

vaccination medicine given to protect against certain diseases

More Books to Read

Burby, Liza. *A Day in the Life of a Mayor: Featuring New York City Mayor Rudy Giuliani*. New York: Rosen Publishing Group, 1998.

Tesar, Jenny E. *America's Top 10 Cities*. Woodbridge, Conn.: Blackbirch Press, Inc., 1998.

Thompson, Gare. *Cities: The Building of America*. Danbury, Conn.: Children's Press, 1997.

Index